# Garden of Things Lost

Published by The Synthesis Center Press
Amherst, Massachusetts
ISBN 978-0-9909590-2-1

Library of Congress Control Number: 2021949523

Cover photograph by Karen Sims
Photograph of author by Nancy Dobbs
Design and technical editing by Ted Slawski

For Damion

# CONTENTS

see you
see you
in a couple of soons
he said
language blooming
on the bud of his tongue

# I

## What We Remember

# Legacy

My father made a picture album before his death.
Black and white photographs with scalloped edges
of two families, children of Polish/Austrian immigrants.

No pictures of their youth spent in the orphanage on a hill.
No photos of grandparents.

No telling of alcohol, botched abortions, early deaths
and ruptured families. Orphans and strays, fostered,
adopted, lost to secrets and separation.

But there is my mother in her early twenties,
pretty, a simple smile in every picture,
no suggestion of the sadness shivering under her skin.
And my father, good looking, a smoky sexual energy,
staring back at me from before I was born.

Men in Navy uniforms.
Snapshots of Army tents, palm trees clustered behind them.

Newspaper clippings of my father's brother,
photo of my mother's brother, both lost to the Pacific,
their youth swallowed by war, gone into dark waters.

Weddings and babies, Uncle Pete in his fedora,
aunts in flowered dresses and wide pants,
cousins not seen in more than fifty years.
Then my brother in a battered cowboy hat
sitting on steps, solemn and lost even at five.

And there I am, alone on a blanket,
my head engulfed by a huge bonnet, eyes serious
looking out from the silence of a photograph.

# Clara and Mary

My grandmothers,
immigrants from Eastern Europe,
spent weeks at sea in the dark stench
of steerage aboard steamships.
They waited in long lines
at the counters of Ellis Island,
trying to understand
the strange tongue asking questions
through impatient interpreters,
clutching their cloth suitcases,
tying and retying babushkas under their chins.
Landing cards pinned to their best clothes.

There were no fine teacups
in their future or husbands
with education and money in the bank.
Their dreams of America disappeared
into the cold water flats of tenements,
diphtheria, drunkenness
and too many hungry children.
Clara dead at 29. Mary gone at 60.

Secrets and shame
stitched forward and back
like shadows down a road
whose name I never knew.
My mother suffered
her relentless sadness,
my father his abandoned,
motherless heart.
And I, a grandmother now,
writing through a long winter,
thinking of Clara and Mary,
who crossed the ocean so long ago.

# Poetry

It came
one spring morning
in the abandoned
orchard
of my childhood,
while I sat high
in a gnarled apple tree.
It was there
in the white blossoms
drifting like flakes of late snow,
on the wind,
breathing against the leaves,
against my face.
I thought
I could hear blood
through veins
of the old tree,
run quick through my own heart.

I didn't know
I was called to be of earth,
of words and wandering.
That somewhere a book
had opened,
with the taste
of that spring light.
My mother
might stand vacant and lost,
starring
out the kitchen window,
but I would have
something that was mine.
Something that sang
inside of me,
something she could not touch,
that no one could take away.

# Lost Poem

Once there was a poem
about a young nun and a girl.
How they walked together on a dirt road,
the sun sinking orange
through a stand of white birch,
leaves a shiver of sundown.
Campers and nuns had been picking
blueberries in a far field.
The early evening was hot with July
and the girl was itchy with dried sweat,
tired, a little homesick
but smitten with the nun.

Weren't there horses in that poem?
Two grey horses watching,
nickering as the nun and the girl passed by?
Weren't the other girls running ahead,
their laughter a ripple in the air,
golden dust kicked up by their shoes?
Didn't they call out to her to catch up?

But she stayed behind,
walking as close to the nun as she could.
The one it would break her heart
to leave at summer's end.
The one she would never forget.
Once there was a poem
about a young nun and a girl,
talking quietly about all the things
the girl never told her mother.
But the nun is dead now.
The girl grown old.
That poem never found.

# Music Never Heard

The old Renault leaked feeble heat
as we drove the New Haven Streets,
leaving the Chinese gift shop where
she'd bought me brass wind chimes
for Christmas.
The December afternoon was raw,
light leaning towards darkness.
On the radio the weatherman said
the needle-like rain would soon
turn to snow, perhaps back to rain.
No promise of a white Christmas.
No promises at all.

The President was dead less than a month
and we stumbled through our senior year,
listening to Baez and Dylan,
trying to make sense of it all.
My life had no idea of itself.
But she was music
I had never heard—
the girl from a private school
who drank Norwegian beer,
read Camus and Buber,
smelled of oil paints,
a body odor, dark, moist.

On the way home snow swallowed sky,
came wet and thick,
crowded the headlights.
In my driveway we talked long and close.
It was night.  It was white. I trembled.
Snow deepened, everything was quiet as sleep.
*Stay*, I said. *The roads are bad.*
*My mother won't mind.*
That night we hung those delicate chimes
from the overhead light in my ceiling,
until one day while I was gone,
my mother threw them away.

# Learning to Drive

One spring afternoon of my senior year,
in our push button Dodge Dart,
my father gave me my first driving lesson.
He took me down a winding road,
grabbed the wheel,
slammed his foot on mine.
I had not braked hard enough,
he said.

We pulled into a small sandy area
along a stream, turned off the car.
He lit an unfiltered Camel.
We opened the windows,
a musty smell of water drifted in.
Red-wing black birds called with
scratchy voices in the soft green willows,
cattails along the banks.

It was a year of assassination and grief
and I had fallen in love
with a new girl at school.
The sin of it stuffed in my throat,
where its pain followed me
across fields of secrets,
before I finally unlocked my shame.

But that afternoon I sat inside
our silence
and my father's unopened heart.
The stream rushing on,
spring sunlight dancing
on its riffled back.
Black birds telling me stories
I could not yet understand.

# August 1969

*for Stephen after all these years*

We were driving back from Texas
in an old beat up Volvo wagon.
Sleeping in the car. Eating Dinty Moore
beef stew heated in a can on an open fire,
along some sleepy brown river in Arkansas.
In a week you were leaving for an Air Force
hospital in Thailand and we were on our way
to a music festival in upstate New York.
Tickets cost $18.00 for the weekend.
In the New York Times ad, a dove sat on a guitar
promising three days of peace and music.

We slowly made our way north and east,
stopping after dark in the Smokey Mountains.
Our car parked in a campsite by a stream,
lantern and fire light soft on the banks,
smell of burning wood singing the night.
We hadn't been married a year and now
your looming absence was everywhere.

That Friday, on the road to the festival,
there were cars and people as far as one could see.
We parked in a wide field above the grounds.
Overhead, helicopters thwupped, carried performers
back and forth, while below a sea of bodies formed
as night fell over the day, stage lights illuminating
Tim Harden, Ravi Shankar, Arlo Guthrie.

Sometime after midnight we fell asleep to rain
thrumming the car roof. I woke later to your
quiet snoring, thought of your leaving,
no awareness how much would shift,
how you would change, how I would
become someone else in your absence.
In the rain, I left the car to pee,
could hear Joan Baez in the distance

singing *Swing Low, Sweet Chariot.*
Her clear voice, liquid in the rainy darkness,
my heart sad, your innocence asleep in the car.
On the other side of the world,
the relentless slapping of helicopters blades
carried bodies of the wounded and the dead.

# All Lost

In the summer of 1970 we moved to a duplex
near the end of Lake Metacomet,
the water only a few yards from our front door,
the swamp smelling of sulfur and mud.

The upstairs neighbor returned from war,
his peace flag flying off the porch railing,
constantly blasted Led Zeppelin, Pink Floyd;
smoking the potent Thai Stick
he'd smuggled back from Viet Nam.

I don't remember his name—Lenny or Benny.
He had a wife who was never home, not even at night
when the murky water licked and stained the sand.

My husband was back from Southeast Asia too,
fungus on his chest, flushing bright red
when he smoked the marijuana he brought home.
Both men had nightmares: bridges on fire, bodies in bags.
Both men had forgotten who they used to be.

Winter arrived, we could no longer hear his music,
only muffled crying above our bedroom ceiling.
The lake froze early, ice an inky deep, no snow,
only cold, a relentless cold.

Some nights I would go out alone into the dark,
stars blazing, bitter light fallen and lost in the
black of the lake. I would lie down on the ice,
pitch stones, rocks, anything I could heave,
listen to the ping and knocks,
the long, lonely thudding across all that was frozen.

# What We Remember

There is a lake in her memory,
long, wide, deep.
There is a guide boat on the water,
water as still as the space between
one breath and another,
until a fish jumps for insects
hovering over the face of the lake,
leaving a ring, a ripple.
There are two women in the boat,
voices soft with the dusky evening air.
Oars nearly silent as they fall then rise,
water dripping off their edges.
There is a pair of loons,
shadowed as light slowly weakens.
V trails across the lake's surface
as they separate, call out
a quiet hoot, a tender yodel.
There are three blond children
waiting on the shore,
with voices like a sighing wind.
A golden puppy is with them.
They are all so young,
the children and their mothers,
their happiness.
There is a lake in her memory.
It's image flawless, haunting.
Children calling their mothers
to come ashore, their flashlights blinking
into the swelling Adirondack night.
Smell of balsam as a mist rises,
far off sound of loon voices,
an eerie echo moving further away,
floating down the arm of the lake.

# Her Secret

She tries not to remember her past,
voices of her Sisters praying softly at Vespers,

while outside the chapel windows
darkness approached with its own song.

She tries to forget how she loved
one of her Sisters with her whole heart,

loved in a way only a young woman can,
all fire in her blood.

She tries not to remember because
she's afraid her husband might suspect

she never loved him the way she loved
someone she never touched,

though for more than forty years she's
enjoyed the hard pleasure of his body,

given him fine, healthy sons,
had a house of men to care for,

been happy in her marriage,
had a life she would call good.

But now she finds herself staring out
the kitchen window to summer trees

nodding green against a faraway sky.
She tries not to think about seventy years gone,

or all that might have been,
if she had only spoken.

# On the Train to Convent Station

A train rumbles along the tracks,
so much time caught under the wheels,
so much breath
mingled with the cold stars.
On the other side of the window
darkness pulls away toward the woods
where fox and deer, sparrows
hunch against an approaching storm.
The train shudders with memory,
a sadness that rumbles
through the night,
sits next to her
as she watches the snow close in,
the darkness deepen.
She pulls beads from her pocket,
old and blessed,
worn with worry,
black as the sky outside.
She can't remember
when she fingered them last,
why they have waited quietly in a drawer,
asking for nothing,
only waiting with patience,
like breath,
like the exhale she made so long ago,
merged now with the breath of Christ
or an owl hoot in the hemlock,
all the nuns softly praying.
The train moves on through the woods,
blows the whistle once,
a long wail into the silence of snow
that keeps falling like breath,
the last exhale of the dead,
time under the wheels.

# Swallows

My brother tells me about thousands of swallows living
on Goose Island near the mouth of the Connecticut River.

He tells me how they arrive each evening,
a dense black cloud as the light begins to die,

how they descend, a swarming funnel, falling like
smoke, disappearing into reedy marsh to roost.

When night presses its shoulder over the water,
the sky is empty of their wing sounds, their liquid chirp.

I swallow what I want to say to my brother.
Swallow years of never having him hear me.

I think of the birds coming together, of how they must listen
to one another as they fall into the dwindling light,

how they murmur and nudge each other, dream of migration.
Five hundred thousand soft breaths in the darkness.

# Birthday Party

There is something about another birthday that makes you stop
between one breath and the next and wonder how you arrived here.

You draw a frayed sweater over your breasts, hold it tight
for a moment and wonder if anyone is looking, if anyone else

knows you feel a clutch in your chest where your heart beats.
The Medicare bill comes in the mail and a new ache emerges

somewhere deep in the gut and you can't spend as many hours
splitting, hauling and stacking firewood as you used to.

You want to think perhaps it's all in your head, you know you're
growing older and the knowing slows you down, but then

the realization, it's your body that's changed, its muscle tone,
sharpness of hearing. Whose face is looking back at you in the mirror?

You remember how you used to go out into the fields alone at night,
everything aching with silence, until a breeze stirred the leaves

to speak and you dreamed you knew what they were saying. You
thought about who you were, who you might become while the stars

arranged a canopy overhead and you pulled down their cold light,
not quite believing how far away they were, that some of those stars

were dead already even though you could see them. The wind would
come again, the blue hoot of an owl would follow and you could not

have dreamed of getting old, your parents dying, children not yet born
becoming middle-aged one day. Here you are at your birthday party,

gripping the sweater, trying to recall what your body felt like when it
hummed with desire and all you could think of was touching her,

waiting to feel her body sing in your mouth, the energy, exquisite magic.
But in this moment you want to break wide open, feel yourself loosen

inside a rush of wind, as you imagine what it might be like
to leave the earth of your body, disappear into a wake of stars

# Dream
### for Damion

A man sits down in the sand on the shore of a lake,
a lake hidden in the folds of the Adirondacks.
The lake, blue and clear, ripples in an east wind.
He squints into the sun, into light singing on the water.
*I came here as a boy*, he says to his two sons.
They say nothing. They squint like their father.

He remembers forty years ago like his own breath,
a half-dream, something he had and lost,
those happy summers vanished.

The sons rise and run together along the shore, laughing
and calling to each other. No one else is around and the man
wonders how he arrived here, down a long dirt road,
the one it felt like forever to drive when he was a boy,
sitting in the back seat with two girls and his dog.

He remembers sleeping on a porch, the nights cool, eerie
wavering call of loons, their laughter and mournful hoot.
He can hear them still, although he never heard them again.

He sees himself in his eldest son, the one skipping rocks across
the face of the water. He wonders how so much time could have
passed while he wasn't looking. How he managed to find this
place, how it feels unchanged, if he is really here at all.
He's not sure if what he remembers is true, all the memories
he has held in his heart for years.

*We have to go*, he yells to the boys. *We shouldn't even be here.*
They turn in unison at the sound of his voice, drop their heads,
walk slowly back to him. They will climb into the car, drive the
road around East Pond Mountain without saying a word.
The boys wait on their father's long silence. The man waits
on what he remembers.

# Eight Years Gone

*for Ashley*

In the faltering light of December,
autumn lies breathless in the garden.

I think of you, mark time by your death,
and cross a narrow bridge into a blue meadow.

I hear you asking me to make your favorite lunch:
grilled cheddar cheese, Campbell's tomato soup.

You pepper the soup until the surface is black,
soak pieces of sandwich in the broth.

Smiling, you say, *"Thank you, my Puya."*
Oh, to call back time before

the warm relief of a needle
took the sadness from your heart.

The light today is long and sweet.
I can see you now, eyes closed,

raising your face to the sun.

# II

## The Sophie Poems

# The Sophie Poems

## *First Day*

She is alone at a metal chain link fence. There are other girls near
but Sophie can't look at them straight on, only a sideward glance,

as if she has only one eye. Her stomach feels as if she swallowed
something heavy and greasy. Afraid she might vomit on her shoes,

the new ones they gave her, black and too big, when she arrived
at this place, this massive dark brick building, rising up on the top

of Highland Avenue, with dozens of gaping glass eyes.
She came in the back seat of a strange car with two of her brothers.

Johnny and Al are still at home. She cannot remember where Joey is.
Home is a dark, cold-water flat, hollow cupboard, empty drawers,

a father drunk, every nickel gone to the wine her mother cries about.
Papa roars, swearing in Polish, spits as he swells Mama's eye shut,

splits her lips, kicking furniture, threatening with closed, enormous fists.
All of them cowering like a litter of frightened kittens.

Now Sophie is alone in the strange place where all the women are
wearing long black dresses, black and white cloth on their heads.

Voices of the girls near her are a loud clanging in her ears, her chest,
her head. And her brothers, her brothers somewhere she cannot see.

## Next Morning

Sophie slept in the same bed as her brothers, Eddie and Stanley.
In winter, heat from the kitchen coal stove barely reached their

windowless back room. It leaked an oily, smoky smell. Soaked into
her sleep where she dreamed of horses she had only seen in pictures.

This morning she wakes to the metallic slap of a bell, alone in a
narrow bed, in a sea of beds, metal frames lined up row after row.

Her heart is beating wild, like a bird snared in her chest. She hears
coughing, sniffling, a whimper from the bed beside her, watches

a weak sun push its way through yellowed shades. Sophie hides
her face, wants her brothers, wants her mother, wants something,

anything but the panic that grips her. She trembles, terrified
to move, terrified to be with those strange girls again.

Women watching. Wearing black, straps of long beads hanging
on skirts. Heads covered. Stern and disapproving. Whispering.

All the girls are getting up, so she gets out of bed, old wooden floor
cold, creaking under bare feet. She shivers, does what the others do,

watches out of the corner of her eye. She speaks to no one. No one
speaks to her. She wants to call for Eddie and Stanley, but boys

and girls are separated. One of the women in black stands in the
doorway, shouts, *Hurry up, girlies*. Sophie's body is somewhere else.

She remembers Mama crying as they were taken away. Now she is here,
inside this place, inside words she has never heard before. Words she

turns over and over on her tongue, as she hurries with the others into
the bathroom: *Nun. Sister. Dormitory. Orphan asylum. Orphan.*

## Months Later

Sadness rooted. Its dark, slender tendrils coil, burrow deep inside her
with a blue she does not understand. Sophie has seen her brothers
          briefly on

Sundays, visiting day, the only time siblings of the opposite sex are al-
lowed to be together. No one has visited, not Mama or Papa, and she
          wonders what

terrible thing they have done to be abandoned here. The children have
been given a piece of paper to write three things they might want for
          Christmas.

She wants to go home but thought a new hair brush would be nice or
roller skates. There is a Christmas tree in the court yard, carol singing
          and talk of baby Jesus.

The nuns have been nicer and discipline not so rigid, although she was
smacked with Sister Angela's strap for reading after lights were turned
          off in the dormitory.

The palms of her hands are red welts, hurt when she makes a fist. But she
wanted to finish <u>The Boxcar Children</u>, four orphans living inside a train
          car in a forest,

until rescued by their grandfather. Sophie has no grandfather, does not
know what one is. Has never seen a real forest or a train car. Maybe she
          could get another one

of their books for Christmas. She writes down *Boxcar Children book, hair
brush, roller skates*. Who will give them to her, she wonders. Will Mama
          and Papa come?

It is almost bedtime. Sister Angela took her book and flashlight away
the night she was strapped. Stanley had given them to her. She wishes
          she could show

her hands to him. Wishes she could disappear. She is afraid all the time. Sad. Can't get the sad out of her. The tree and singing only make it
worse. Sophie

thinks about running away, maybe to a forest, but she doesn't know where she is or how to find where she used to live. She only knows she
is heavy and light

at the same time, has found a place inside herself where she can go and hide. A close dark place. A shadow place with no voice but her own.

# Fostered

Sophie has a home now, but not with Mama and Papa. She is with the good doctor and his family, in a fancy house, vast green yard with tulip trees and

red flowers. No brick building with glass eyes. No cement playground. But her brothers are lost to her now. She feels misplaced in a kind of picture-book

story with a real family but not her family. She is old enough to work, comes home right after school to do laundry, ironing, cleaning. Looks after three children.

She has a bedroom all to herself, with a pretty soft bed, night table. A chair and a desk by a window that welcomes morning light. Absent the rows of metal

bed frames, the coughing and crying of other girls. No more dark nuns watching their mouths speaking of sin and punishment. The mother of the house is rarely home,

gives instructions, clothes and feeds her well but offers little. No hugs. No kind words. She has Poco. Pretends the dog is hers. Huge, slobbering, affectionate Saint Bernard.

She steals minutes from her afternoon chores to be alone with him behind the trees in the great back yard, where she buries her face in his fur, humming.

But sometimes after she goes to bed, the good doctor comes to her, touches her in places she does not want to be touched. He whispers, softly, kindly,

*Shhh now. Don't you tell.* Then disappears into the darkness of the night-house, a ghost. She lies there trembling, her mind hidden in a corner of the ceiling.

One night, as she whimpers under his hands, Poco comes into her bedroom. Stands huge beside her, nudges and licks her, makes a low moan, a growl,

turns to his master with a vicious snarl and snaps. The man of the house never returns to her bed. Never looks her in the eyes again.

# 1943

Sophie is free, free of indentured service, the family that did not love
her, free of the dark nuns with their murmurs and incantations. She has
      a room

to herself in the YWCA, good job working in an aircraft factory. Takes a
bus to work, eats her meals at the Automat, hordes tea,
      jam, biscuits.

Her country is at war, a terrible war. Stanley is fighting somewhere in the
South Pacific. Her beloved Eddie is already dead. Eighteen years old and

gone to lie at the bottom of an ocean. She missed so much of their lives.
Missed so much of her own and still has bad dreams about the good
      doctor.

Sophie wants to find her mother, the other brothers lost to the terror of
time. She has an address but it is in another state. Stanley gave it to her
      before he

left for the Army. He said their father was dead. Died of pneumonia after
passing out drunk in a gutter. She keeps the paper folded neatly in her

underwear drawer, too troubled in her heart to actually find her way
there. Someday soon, she thinks, but what would she say after all these
      years of silence?

She is a pretty young woman, soft and sad, carries sadness deep inside
bone. She has a few girl friends who work with her at the plant, dated a
      friend of Stanley's

a few times, but he is away on an aircraft carrier on a nameless sea. He
was in the orphanage too, watched her through the same chain link
      fence that separated boys

from girls. His name is Paul. She remembers his smoky handsome-ness,
receives an occasional letter. He feels like a brother, someone she might
      be able to love.

But she has a hole in her somewhere, a hole dark and deep. Some-times she finds herself staring out a window, waiting for something that never seems to come.

# III

## What Finds Its Way Into a Poem

# Hartford to Albuquerque

By the time we arrived
we had been awake nearly forty hours.
Trapped inside planes and airport terminals,
no fresh air except for a brief walk
across the tarmac in Grand Junction,
where half the sky was raven black,
the other blue with a piece of rainbow in its corner.

*Cancelled to Dallas*
*Delayed in Charleston.*
*Denver shut down.*
*Diverted to Grand Junction.*
*Stranded back in Denver.*
*Leaking hydraulic fluid at 30,000 feet outside of Phoenix.*
*Emergency landing.*

The successions of weather and mechanical calamities
struck us, knocked us over,
sat between my eyes like heavy grit.
Bad food.
Soiled clothes.
No luggage.
Trying to sleep on an airport floor.
My feet hurt, smelled so bad,
I thought something had died inside my shoes.
*What must it feel like to be a refugee*, I asked her.
Our lost, wandering hours
only a swallow of belonging nowhere.

Finally arrival in Albuquerque.
Negotiating a rental car as rain splattered on us,
as thunder ripped over the Sandia Mountains.
Exhaustion stuck to our skin, hot, viscous.
with more than two hours left to drive,
both of us on the edge of forgetting who we were.
Interstate 40, speed and tractor-trailer trucks
and a blinding sun sinking low into the western sky.

# Wild Sheep Place

An elk kept us awake
most of the night,
bugling into the darkness
under a black sky
crowded with stars.
We could not see him
across the canyon floor,
only hear the sound
of his low, throaty grunt,
followed by a high,
hoarse whistle,
then silence.

Wild Sheep Mesa slept.
So did ancient buttes,
discarded pottery shards,
broken adobe walls and
ponderosa pines on the hillside.
We tossed, turned,
flipped our pillows
as night passed.
In the morning
the sun rose like gold
from behind the Zuni Mountains,
the sky clear as god's eye

# What Finds Its Way into a Poem

On our way to see the return
of sand hill cranes and snow geese
at the Bosque del Apache Refuge,
we pull off Interstate 25
about twenty miles north
of Socorro, New Mexico.

It's an isolated truck stop,
surrounded by nothing
but sparse vegetation,
yellow and red sandstone.
A homeless woman,
in the company of four dogs,
squats over a knotted bundle
tied to a makeshift cart.

The woman looks middle-aged,
strands of hair drift across her face,
a face that betrays nothing
as she looks back at us.
Wind blows red dirt, plastic bags
over the parking lot where semi's idle.
A chill settles into the wide
gray October afternoon.

We wonder where she came from,
where the woman will sleep tonight,
with her cart and her dogs,
her homeless heart.
After we use the bathroom
we turn back on the highway.
For miles a quiet
settles deep between us
until I turn to you and ask,
*Should we at least*
*have given her 20 dollars?*

# Winter Deer

They come,
first one,
then another,
ghosts of dusk,
nudging spindly grasses,
dried seed heads,
mouthing what is left to eat
on drab January earth.
Without a sound
twenty appear,
an apparition as light dies
and shadows swallow
what is left of the day.
Tonight there will be
a brief eyelid of moon
before slipping behind
the canyon wall
as dark
overtakes itself.
I imagine them
going off to sleep
in the shallow
wide-mouthed cave,
sheltered on dry red sand
made soft by time.
I can hear their
breath gently huffing
in the black night.

# Welcome to Taos

A late dinner in a strange town.
The light beyond the walled garden
lazy, lovely, seductive
and the dead-end road
calls you out for a walk.
The two of you are happy,
talking softly into the blushing air,
scented by the flowers of Russian Olive trees.

The blunt bark of a dog,
just one bark, startles the heart.
As you turn,
the punch of its mouth
is unexpected, hard.
You pitch forward,
lose your breath,
your whole body shaking.

A Great Dane has ripped your flesh
and disappeared like a black ghost.
You feel blood
soak your underwear,
swallow fear,
stony and bitter in your throat
as you stumble, trembling,
back down the road.

# what can you say

about walking out of one life
and back into another
always something left behind
pieces of white stone
the tiniest rufous feather
a garden of fire flies in July

what is it to fully inhabit a life
one life
perhaps two
to sit on the edge of a wire fence
waiting for sweet water to appear in
an upside down bowl of red

what can you say about someone else's grief
the kind that trembles under every inch of skin

in the darkness of a high desert night
I have heard spade foot toads
sing after a long female rain
and thunder
the way it rolls through the canyon
rumbles into your bones

# Visitor Center on the Way Home

She stood on a slope of hill,
squinted into the Alabama sun.
A pretty woman,
fifty or so, thin,
a flowered shift
falling just above her knees.
She asked us something in Spanish,
weak smile hovering over
a bewildered expression on her face.
No purse, no cell phone,
nothing but a flap of her hands,
asking us something
we could not understand.
Someone at the information desk
told us the woman
had been left behind.
Her ride gone.
But no one there
spoke her language,
no one knew
how she ended up alone
on a sultry summer Alabama morning.

# Jack

I drove past a white vase
filled with gladiolas today.
They were sitting on a wooden table
by the side of the road
and I thought of you, Jack,
you, my poet brother, so far away.
I miss you,
as I do the others.
Our Sunday morning poetry.
All of us sitting at
Inscription Rock Trading Post
drinking tea and coffee
sharing our internal worlds.

You grew lovely gladiolas
in the garden near El Morro,
rows of corn, squash and beans.
You would sit there, watch the
sun slide west as evening crept in
over sage and rabbit brush.
Sky caught in the windows
of your adobe house.
Once you brought me a bouquet
of gladiolas,
red and plum, ginger and white,
placed them near the stage
where I gave a poetry reading.

But age has not been kind to you, Jack.
One of the last times I saw you,
you didn't know why
we were in the Gallery
where Tim and I would celebrate
the publication of our new books of poetry
Couldn't find your keys,
didn't know where the car was.
And the next morning

when we met for breakfast,
I asked you about planting the gladiolas.
*I don't have enough time*, you answered

# Two Places

We talked for days,
months really
about how
to live in two places
at the same time.
One with its fathomless,
hard blue sky,
beauty, dry and harsh,
golden, inaudible light.
The other lush
green farm land,
soft roll of hills,
black and white cows
on wet, foggy mornings.
We walked our road.
We walked our grief.
We choked on all
we did not understand
while unseen owls
called softly in darkness
and black crows sat high
in the old maple tree
calling out their
raspy opinions at dawn.
We talked for days,
months really
until we understood
in our blood
how we had to choose,
knowing the choosing
would break
our already broken hearts.
We left behind red rock,
skinny horses and rangy cattle.

We left behind a primeval light,
so perfect
you swore could see your soul.
We left behind something
we could not take with us.

# IV

## Ott's Farm

# Ott's Farm

## I    Brave and Dreamy Selves

Ott lived on the farm all his life, died before they widened
the road, built an elementary school in his alfalfa field.

Blew his brains out one night in dim kitchen light,
chickens gone, no cows to milk, no wife to keep him warm.

Children walked past the empty barn on their way to school,
heads down, Ott's phantom cows bellowing at milking time.

But a handful of kids, dreamy and brave, didn't care about ghostly cows.
They tramped down a path under the catalpa trees to the crooked barn
    door,

collected long beans on their way, searched for broken and lost things,
anything to use, guard, hide from their parents.

Inside they met silence. The smell of old manure, rotted hay. Spider
webs hanging from the eaves. A hushed owl with lemon eyes.

# II                                        Keepsies

Up behind Ott's old cow barn was a long-abandoned chicken coop,
nesting boxes torn out, hen droppings dry as dust.

Four kids turned it into a place no adults knew of,
a place to keep secrets, share an occasional stolen cigarette.

Ann, Patsie, Tommy and Chuck, none older than ten, friends
since kindergarten, inseparable, rowdy as a litter of pups.

They swept out the coop, white-washed walls, tacked up pages torn
from Dell comic books, Photoplay magazine. Peed in a bucket.

It was rural Connecticut of the 1950's where farmland grew modest
houses after the war. The war their fathers never talked about,

the war they played running, shouting through backyards, when they
weren't shooting cat's eyes and aggies in dusty circles, pots in the dirt.

They ate Twinkies, Stateline Potato Chips, drank bottled Coke, traded
baseball cards that smelled of bubble gum. Carried marbles in white socks,

and rode bikes home to watch American Bandstand before dinner
where they found their mothers, alone, fussy with questions.

Mothers with no language for the emptiness that soaked their days,
no driver's license, no second car, the walk to a bus stop, miles away.

Later, after work, fathers arrived, tired and silent, full of something
the children knew to stay away from. They learned how to hide

small fears, fragments of unspoken needs in their pants pockets
like the few special marbles they would never play for keeps.

# III                    Long Dark and Falling Light

In mid-December the year Ann turned eleven,
cold descended, settled deep and early before snow fell.

The wide, shallow pond across from Ott's deserted
farmhouse froze a cloudy white, while the bordering

swamp with reeds and tufts of grass froze clear like
the bubbled glass in the windows of the old house.

The gang of four, along with other kids, came to his pond
after school to skate, knock a puck around, make small fires

to warm frozen fingers, cold toes. Sometimes there were
hot dogs, marshmallows smuggled from home.

One afternoon Ann skated off alone to the swamp, away from
play and shouts, so she could think, see where painted turtles

rested, nestled in the mud and leaves, not breathing,
hearts barely beating. Mystery lingered long in her mind.

Why didn't they die under all that ice and cold?
Did they dream during their dark winter sleep?

Crows cawed, sharp and raspy from trees at the edge
of the wood. The sky lost its color, dull December light

dwindled toward the dark of solstice, the air sharpened.
Christmas music played on the radio, songs of joy and peace,

songs written during her father's war before she was born.
Ann thought about war and turtles and who God was.

She skated back to the pond, the laughter of her friends,
but she tripped on someone's dropped mitten, slid across the ice

as Tommy also stumbled, his skate blade jamming into her thigh. Pants, blood soaked and torn, she limped home in the falling light.

# IV             End of Summer

Time had pulled them from childhood, from their young
dreamy selves. No one played inside the barn anymore.

The chicken coop had collapsed in on itself. But Ann often walked by
Ott's barn, as she wandered past the elementary school,

down to the pond or up by the old swamp, into the woods
where she would find a place to sit and think.

In a few days most of her graduation class would take
new roads to college, jobs in faraway places, marriage.

She was solitary now, uncertain, had strayed from her childhood
circle, fallen in love with a student new to school. Could not name

the hunger that gripped her, bled under her skin. Did not understand the
grief suffered when her friend went off to Paris with a boy friend.

Ann spoke to no one of her fears, her anguished shame,
the sadness she began to wear like a rough blue cloak.

Fear rendered her tight. She brooded, hid from her mother's gaze,
a gaze that pierced Ann like barbed wire, a look that said:

*I'm glad she left you.*
*I'm glad she is no longer in your life.*

Ann scribbled poems in a notebook carried everywhere,
chanted prayers like a flock of broken stones, heavy in her mouth.

Wished she were eleven again, laughing with Patsie, Tommy and Chuck,
A sock full of marbles, comic book in her hands.

# V                    Goodbye

The light sighed now toward coming darkness. Ann parked
her car off the road, wheels half on the sidewalk, where

she had walked so many years ago, until they had grown, moved
on to life beyond childhood, teenage angst, their parent's houses.

She wondered if she listened hard enough, could she hear the voices of
her friends calling out to each other as they parted for home,

dinner and the shows they watched on black and white TV's. Days of
promises and secrets, when winning at marbles was all that mattered.

Ann knew she was standing in the right place, not far from the corner,
under wide catalpa trees. But the barn was gone, so too Ott's farm house.

In their place, fancy homes, long black driveways, pale trimmed lawns.
Across the road the swamp had been filled in, the shallow pond

smaller then she remembered, now in someone's back yard.
She shivered in the November dusk, found dried heart shaped

catalpa leaves and long beans on the sidewalk. Ann breathed their
names: *Patsie, Tommy, Chuck*. Saw their cheeks flushed with cold,

eyes bright and wide as they discovered some new treasure in corners of
the barn, astonished as an owl looked down from ceiling rafters.

So many years gone. So many miles traveled. Books written.
She had been married to a woman for years now. Lived far away.

Chuck was dead at thirty from AIDS, Tommy missing in Viet Nam,
Patsie disappeared into time. *Is it good to remember*, she wondered,

pulling her collar up against a blue slip of wind. For a moment she
heard their laughter, the low bawl of Ott's cows at milking time, all

whispering in her ears now. A slight smile caught the side of her mouth. Memory and dreams gathering in what remained of the light.

# V

## Hoodlum Dogs of Tulum

# Far From Home

The hotel across the road
falls asleep
window by window.
Darkness in the mouths of glass.
As others lie sleeping
I sit alone on the second floor porch,
sipping vodka and melted ice,
listening to coconut fronds
swimming in the wind.
Coatis emerge
from the dense mangrove.
Bandits of the night,
nosing through trash
for discarded fruit,
carrying off a plastic bag
into the black forest..
The sky is a gauze of clouds,
the moon, drowsy and vague,
sleeps on her back.

# Mexican Boy

On the beach
a barefoot boy
in a red shirt
plays with
a plastic bag.
For an hour
it is
cape
parachute
kite
hat
balloon.
He chases it
tucks it
rolls with it
sits on it
struts across
the beach with it
until tired
he stuffs it
into his jeans pocket.

# Joseph

Late afternoon and the old man pushes
an ancient tricycle with a battered cooler attached.
Inside tamales made by his wife, nestle under
a yellow flowered cloth: pollo, queso, frijoles.

In a weathered face, his smile, big as a dinner plate,
shows a front tooth missing. He recognizes us
from past years, opens his arms for a hug, and
tells me something in Spanish I do not understand.

He lives in old Colonia, a town across Highway 307,
on the other side of the mangrove swamp,
where most of the locals live and work, far
from the resorts on the road to Playa del Carmen.

Together we admire the bougainvillea, two colors
climbing along the top of the wall outside our
condo rental. *Roja*, he says. *Rosado*, he says,
as he turns, smiles again, sings down the street.

# Hoodlum Dogs of Tulum

As twilight gathers in Tulum
a pack of dogs bark down the sun.
They chase hunger,
Mayan ghosts,
they chase each other.
Cries of the scrawny mob come close,
move far away, circle back through side streets
littered with spoiled fruit and cardboard,
a rotten mattress, cracked toilet,
piles of old brittle palm fronds.

Inside the enclosed garden of a tourist hotel,
a Buddha fountain gurgles in the courtyard
where tiled walkways are washed,
swept clean each morning.
Gates locked at 8pm when pool lights
begin to change the water's color.

Outside in the street an old man
on a bicycle squeezes a horn nonstop.
He rides back and forth,
selling something, anything for a few pesos.
As night crawls in over the pueblo,
the man makes one last pass
down the avenue,
the horn sounding over and over.
The hoodlum dogs barking after him,
barking, barking, they do not stop.

# Old Woman

wizened like a corn husk doll
or a bird mummified,
paces the beach every day, begging.
Less than five feet tall,
she wears the same white dress,
white square handkerchief over her head.
Skin dark leather,
eyes hooded in a long face,
bottom teeth protruding.
She wanders slow, deliberate.
If you give her a few pesos,
her eyes meet yours,
a hand flutters up toward heaven
and she gives you a blessing in words
you don't need to understand.
Near the square after dark,
she sits rocking on a concrete stoop,
a heaviness around her.
In the restaurant above,
tourists laugh, drink margaritas,
talk about buying silver jewelry,
weather back home,
listening to panpipe music
drift up from the square.

# Hermes

He waits on the corner,
blue baseball cap pulled down,
orange fingernail polish on one hand,
rosary beads wrapped around wrist
and middle finger of the other.
His energy is soft as he asks us
to try the new restaurant
on the next street over, a small
place off the main road to town.
The street is torn up from a water project,
piles of concrete wait like ruins
by the side of the road.
He walks with us, translating
"full moon over the sea" in Spanish,
reminds us to watch the shift of light
across the water after dinner.
He gathers chairs for a table
on the sidewalk where lights run
blue across the bottom of an awning.
Only men are working here.
The cook needs glasses,
holds each order up close to his face,
where you can see him making dinners
through a crude opening in the wall.
A Bee Gees song plays in the background.
The old waiter catches my eye
and we rock back and forth to the music
before he turns to the cook.
When we leave Hermes is back
standing on the corner,
pointing at the rising swollen moon.

# Puerto Morelos: Winter 2018

A mockingbird sits on an electric wire
mimicking as many birds sounds as he can.
Quiets now, flicks his tale,
surveys the street as the hour approaches five.
Palm fronds constantly sway,
a lazy, slow sway this afternoon.

Outside this walled garden,
with potted crimson hibiscus,
pink bougainvillea, green tiled pool,
all the lovely touches tourists desire,
a third world country lives a few blocks away.
Corrugated or thatched roofs, dirt floors,
chickens scratching in cracked limestone soil.
On a broken sidewalk, a laughing toddler
bathes in a ten-gallon bucket.

I am growing old now,
weary of our beautiful broken world,
fear the coming order of things—
the way truth grows thin, pales,
becomes something forgotten.
But for this moment the mockingbird
takes up singing again and a great-tailed
grackle creaks into the empty blue sky.

# Old Dyke in the Train Station

Snowstorms and cancelled flights.
Stranded in Philadelphia.
We sit in the 30th Street Station,
with its columns and filigree,
statue of Archangel Michael
lifting a fallen soldier
from the ruins of war.
Always a war somewhere.
A pair of house sparrows perch
above the florist stand, hop along the back
of worn wooden benches
where a ragged young man nods off
at the end of our row.
Arrivals and departures call out,
echo in the tall ceilinged room.
There is an echo in my heart
I can't seem to silence,
grown deeper with years,
prayers I've forgotten.
Six hours to wait
before the train heads north,
our Mexican tans already fading.
People come and go. People wander.
Babies wail, children fuss, people embrace,
in a corner an elderly man quietly weeps.
Outside the ladies room
a homeless woman
digging in the trash
mutters under her breath,
and I see myself in the full-length mirror.
*You look like an old country dyke,*
I mutter to myself.
Wrinkled red flannel shirt,
black baggy sweat pants,
too much weight around the waist,
rimless glasses, short hair,
a baseball cap pulled down.

I suddenly feel out of time
and sometimes out of my mind.
Back on the bench, I remember
blossoms of red bougainvillea,
remember when I was young,
and my heart had no echo.

# VI

Garden of Things Lost

# Stumbling after God

If you leave first,
slip through the dark membrane of death,
what would become of me
after all these years?
Would I take my ruined heart,
tuck it deep inside
this chest of muscle and bone,
drive away from these hills
closer to the civilized world?
Or would I stay on alone,
in this place we made home,
mournful, stumbling after God?
Would I pour spirits a little earlier
each day into a tin cup,
listen to the clink of ice against it edge?
Let a small flock of chickens
wander the overgrown yard,
cluck through the kitchen in the afternoon?
Would I invite coyote to sleep
safely under the porch,
call out to raven and wren
to share food at my table?
Would I grow my hair long and wild,
let it tangle with words and feathers,
waiting for time
to catch me off guard,
still my heart in mid-sentence?

# Louie Black

A few years ago, on a late autumn day like this, they took down
the old Black house. Bulldozers and backhoes battered and smashed,

hauled and scraped the earth clean till you would never know a house
and trees had stood there for two hundred years. In the early 1900's

the only sounds on this road were the thud of Louie's splitting maul on
wood, huff of horses, bawling of the neighbor's cows. He lived alone

in the old family farm house and stories tell of a drinking man with an
unhurried smile, who loved his daily solitude, nights down at the village

tavern. Sometimes he would drink so much rum, he'd fall down drunk.
His buddies would lift him into the back of his buck-board. They'd slap

the rump of Louie's horse, who knew the way home, up Couch Brook Rd.
Louie would sleep it off until the sun came up and crows called him awake.

Today where the house stood is grassy pasture. Trees gone, Couch Brook Rd.
only a rutted trench. Across the pasture sits a huge house, radiant heat in

the floors, cathedral ceilings, a dozen windows on the world. Fancy horses
in the field. But on a morning like this Louie would still recognize the turn

of his old road, with Long Woods and the hills folding to the east. He might
tell of watching the last catamount disappear into the trees.

# Winter Psalm

Outside our window,
the morning spoke to me
of rumpled time, rivers of light.
Snow was heavy on winter branches
and blue broke through clouds
turning another page in the sky.

*I am more than I know myself to be,*
I said to the glass,
where doves on the other side
pecked at black seed,
looked back at me as though I were not there.

Wind kicked at the branches
and clots of snow fell.
Doves left the ground in a burst of wings
to rest like prayers in the wild cherry tree.

After a storm twenty winters ago,
we would have spent the morning
shoveling to the goats and chickens,
hauling buckets of warm water,
sweet smelling grain.

We might have come back to the house,
to touch under flannel sheets,
singing into each other's bodies,
drifting off to sleep.

But those days are gone,
remembered under the skin,
behind these eyes looking out
at the white dancing fields,
the morning still telling me stories,
time trembling like a psalm.

# Blueberries in March

*That's the last of them*, I say,
bringing the quart package
up from the basement.
They are nestled together,
cold and blue,
frozen with a slight covering of frost.
I put some in a shallow bowl
on the woodstove
to thaw for morning yogurt.
The sky outside already clouded.
Wind batters the trees
and tiny finch feet cling
to the feeder swinging back and forth
on a skeleton branch of the witch hazel.
We picked these berries in late July,
kept safe under tobacco netting
from the beak of a watchful catbird.
The berries were warm with sun then,
sweet and generous on the bushes.
We ate some, froze the rest so we
could take summer out of the freezer,
remembering the twitter of nesting tree swallows,
or the color of our granddaughter's eyes
when she rode your shoulders so long ago.

# About Loneliness

For weeks a ring-necked pheasant has taken up residence
in the abandoned cow pasture behind our house.

Flash of brilliant red on his face. Pure white ring at his neck.
He emerges from a tangle of brush, calls and calls, fluffs feathers,

walks back and forth, through his crowing ground, waiting for a hen
to arrive. Days later and no hen has answered him.

And all winter, a solitary Carolina wren came to the suet every day,
amidst pairs of woodpeckers, nuthatches, cardinals.

Wren is gone now. Gone into this season not winter, not spring,
odd half-time of in-between light, of mud and madness, while migrating

birds return, only to sing once or twice then disappear on a sharp wind.
Month of cruelty, nothing but false starts and longing, sickness in our
          house

and the news of an old poet-friend's death from far away. His body,
weightless as a winged creature, wrapped in white, carried by men who
          loved him.

Soon a deeper spring will emerge. The light will hum. But the pheasant
with his handsome face, what will become of him? What of little
          cinnamon colored wren?

# Making Bread

Her hands smell of honey and yeast,
the kitchen warmed by the woodstove.
Outside, a cold spring rain soaks the world green.
She's making bread this morning
while the stove breathes and the rain falls.
She knows she is more fortunate than so many,
living in her house on the hill.
No bombs, no starvation,
no tent flapping in parched sandy wind.
She is not clutching papers at a fence,
seeking asylum after the rape and beating
she suffered in the dying forests of her home.
No, she is stands in the kitchen watching
an oriole fill his beak with suet,
while she carefully kneads yeasty dough
before putting it in a blue bowl by the stove.
In her bones she does not know evil or desolation
but her mind understands its grip on history,
its ever present malignancy,
the darkness hiding in the hearts of good people.
But for now the gray cat stretches and moans
on the rug near the stove
and rain falls quietly outside her window.

# April Litany: 2018

Two days of sun in twenty,
gray pulls down inside a drum, sealed tight.

In the parking lot of the medical center, your partner locks
her keys in the car and you are called to rescue,
even though you're sick, coughing like an old mongrel
and it's raining as if it's the end of the world.
Wild, drenched to the skin, you drive to Greenfield
nearly sliding off the road in four inches of sodden snow.

Your seven year old granddaughter wants to be a boy,
change her name, has cut off her long hair,
loves looking handsome, no clue the gravity of her want.

The hard drive on your laptop crashes
and you have to send it to Texas for a fix.
How many poems may be wounded beyond recognition?

But wait the month isn't over yet.

The doctor declares you have inflammatory arthritis,
wants you to take an anti-malarial drug that could
stop your heart or render you blind and your partner's
oral surgery has left her face bruised, swollen
as if someone had beaten her.

You both feel you've been robbed of something vital,
left orphaned to die on the side of a muddy road.

The President tweets. The notes are leaked.

The hated house sparrows grin from atop the nesting box.
You plot ways to murder them before they kill the bluebirds.
But try not to worry too much. The birds will take care
of themselves, grass and leaves will soon swell a tender green.
Perhaps the king will be dethroned.

So, pour a drink. Forget it's been cloudy for nearly
twenty days. It doesn't matter now anyway.
It's night. It's dark outside.
Just remember not to eat of the darkness.

# First Cutting

*Where I grew up in Iowa there were meadowlarks everywhere.
Now there are no meadows.* Ann McNelly

The farmer parked his tractor
near the top of the driveway.
Odd, only the first week of June,
not early July when he always
runs his first hay mowing.

Bobolinks sway on blades of grass,
effortless balance,
then a burbling laughing call
as a male takes flight across the field,
his black and white tuxedo
coming to rest in a branch by the road.

Days pass, the tractor remains idle.
Late one afternoon it rumbles, spits smoke,
smell of diesel fuel rides the air
as it starts across the field,
old sickle bar mower pulled along.

Bobolinks lift up from the meadow nests.
Cries caught in small throats,
unheard under the tractor's growl.
After half the field is cut the farmer leaves.
Sweet smell of timothy, alfalfa and clover.

Soon crows drop down black,
prance and swagger between the rows.
Bobolinks frantically circle,
calling, calling, crying into the air.

# Things We Do Not Tell

You two have come to our house again,
the house that sits on top of a hill,
the place with gardens
and long walks in the woods.
Horses pasture up the dirt road.
Our home is not far from a river
where I tell you about the water's current
and what minnows are. About Elliot's house
smashing to pieces against the bridge in a storm,
then floating away down this river
you play in today, throw stones across,
remembering where the water is too deep.

Late afternoon we go up to the garden.
Your small hands in the dirt
feeling fat potatoes hiding,
the surprise on your faces when you find one,
like treasure, a prize in the earth.

After dinner and ice cream, baths finished,
pajamas on, dusk crawls in over August light.
Summer sighs.
I load up the car with wet river shoes,
toys you brought from home and
bags filled with new school clothes.
Far away children have empty stomachs,
their school and homes in rubble.
You know nothing of this and I do not tell.
I buckle you into your booster seats and before
we cross the town line, you are both asleep,
dreaming of things I can only imagine.

# Dayne, Sitting by the Fire

They went out,
just the two of them,
to sit by the campfire
as the late summer light
chased itself home.
He was in his basketball pajamas,
shoes with no socks,
hair damp from a bath.
He shivered.
She took off her fleece vest,
draped it over his small shoulders.
An owl hooted far off
and he asked why,
why it made that noise.
She answered and he nodded,
leaned closer to the fire,
his face illuminated by the flames.
He wondered what kind of monsters
might be hiding in the woods,
especially now that the dark
swelled up all around them.
No light but the flicker of the fire,
no sound except their voices,
the crickets,
hoot of an owl.

# On the Eve of Your Name Change
### *for Dylan*

Even before language found your tongue,
you knew something was wrong.
Pulled at the collar of your blouse,
cried when they put a dress on you.
Wanted your brother's things,
because nothing felt true,
exiled within your own body.
Four years old, one Christmas Eve,
you thumped your chest twice and said,
*My god made me a boy.*
We knew then
the sky would shatter above you someday,
your young haunted self would shake off
the false claim your body made,
your voice would lift with longing
to say you wanted everyone to call you *he*,
call you Dylan John not Emmalina Sophia.
At nine years old your parents still hold your hand
proud of your brave heart,
knowing even in your fearless certainty,
you stand on the edge of a wide meadow,
where monsters wait in the woods.
And as you wander through an undefined geography,
we would spare you any anguish if we could,
knowing in time, sorrow finds us all.
But for now you are a boy running through childhood,
running with a name you gave yourself.

# Girls on the Hill

is what neighbors called them,
two aging women singing
each other's song for thirty years.
And they've sung that song
as birds arrive, depart
humming their own hymns
in the green leafed trees.
Chickens and goats long gone,
a companionship of shadow,
like the dogs they once loved
or the granddaughter whose death
ripped a hole in the air,
leaving them breathless and broken,
while the sun still rose orange behind
a fold of eastern hills
and the corn grew tall,
raspy in late summer wind.
What are the women called now
as their days grow shorter
like autumn's turn of time,
like wild bees asleep in purple asters?
Summer gasps,
exhales its diminishing light
across fields and trees
while October dances in
with its own kind of light.
Soon enough the letting go will come
with its moan and shudder,
a chorus of wind and hollow-boned wings.
Two women alone on a hill
singing of seed, soil, stone, sky.

# Farm at the End of the Road

The farm house is abandoned,
condemned
and the grown children have come
to pick over its bones
Discarded baler, rusty hay rakes,
1950 Ford tractor the old man loved,
all sit patiently behind the barn.
Two draft horses stand
in silver November light.
They shiver,
eye the strangers with their ears,
turn wide backs on them,
waiting for familiar voices.

Like fruit, ghosts of laughter
cling to branches of a failing apple tree
where a wooden swing once hung.
Now all is left to silence,
heart of the tree gone,
trunk hollowed,
composting itself.

A bedroom ceiling is rain-soaked,
mold blooms black
on peeling flowered wallpaper,
smells of rotted plaster,
a dank animal stink where
raccoons have nested in the closet.
Quiet rests in the dry, neat kitchen.
A wood cook-stove
shelters mice in soft layers of milkweed.
Chipped blue plates wait on the table
where the old woman left them
and for a moment the children pause,
listen to something they cannot hear.

Leaving, they stand by their cars,
speak of the coming auction,
of who will care for the horses till then.
Doors slam and dust
rises from the dirt road as they drive away.
November light pales.
The horses wander up a hillside.

# Leavings

How to say goodbye to something
that breathes your blood,
has sustained you for thirty years?
Distant views, the long nourishing
of eye and imagination—
a bowl of sky
in the dark of night
with its soak of swarming stars,
or the moonrise, riding an eastern sky,
full or wobbled just outside the window glass?

Clouds sail like time,
like words across parchment,
a taut pull of grief.

Tree swallows will return
without us this spring,
so too faithful phoebe
and a pair of blue birds.
Daffodils will push through old snow
and chives will reach for warming sun.
But we will be away from this hill
with its wide winds,
hay fields of alfalfa and clover,
howl of coyotes and an enduring solitude.

Clouds sail like feathers on a river,
like the inevitable leavings of time,
an exhale of letting go.

# In my mind I make a garden

of what has been lost.
Sunflowers of our republic gone to ruin
a plague upon us,
weeds of memory, forgotten splendor.

"The art of losing" Elizabeth Bishop called it.
An art we are forced to practice,
grief of endings, of leavings:
parents gone, dogs dead,
a grandchild lost to a needle in her arm.

In other places, other times, even now,
bombs fall and birds die in the trees,
gardens and crops wither and perish,
locusts darken the sky.
How did we think we could
be sheltered from our own ruin?

I made a garden of things lost
as weeds grow unchecked,
as night beetles eat away at democracy,
as people die every day from an terrible virus.

I once wore nuns' clothes next to my skin.
Fell asleep to the yodel of loons on a north woods lake.
I had land I loved and lost,
took long walks on a road of red dust.
I had a young body that sang under the touch of her mouth.
All gone now like a rundown clock and the rule of law.

Grief and rapture, knowing you will
lose everything you have ever loved
until you lose yourself as well,
until you fall into the eye of time,
blessed as a long night carries you home.

# Acknowledgements

Acknowledgement is made to the editors of the journals in which the following poems appeared:

*Silkworm II*: "Puerto Morelos: Winter 2018"; *Tipping the Scales*: "What we Remember", "Music Never Heard", "Winter Psalm", "Far From Home"; *Journal of the Association of the Advancement of Psychosynthesis*: "On the Eve of Your Name Change", *Naugatuck River Review* "Swallows". "Brave and Dreamy Selves"first appeared in a slightly different form in <u>What Sleeps Inside</u> by the author.

In gratitude to all who had a part in the creation of this collection: The Friday Morning Poets for their ongoing support; Susie Patlove for her careful editing; Tom Davis for his encouragement and generous comments, and many thanks to Margo Fleck and Abigail Warren for their reading and feedback on these poems; Didi Firman for her friendship and always a special thank you to Karen for her loving support, intuitive editing and our journey together.

www.ingramcontent.com/pod-product-compliance
Lightning Source LLC
Chambersburg PA
CBHW020949090426
42736CB00010B/1335